No One Cares

No One Cares...

Copyright © 2024 by Page Cole
This title is also available as an eBook from Amazon.com

Pictures are AI generated using a cartoon version of myself as the basis!

All rights reserved. No part of this publication may be reproduced, stored in a retrieval system, or transmitted in any form or by any means - electronic, mechanical, photocopy, recording, or any other - except for brief quotations in printed reviews, without the prior permission of the publisher.

Introduction

This fun little book is intended to be 3 things:

Satire- Satire is defined as the use of humor, irony, exaggeration or ridicule to expose and criticize people's stupidity or vices, particularly in the context of contemporary politics and other topical issues. Lighten up my friends...

Comedy- Everyone of us deserves to have someone poke fun at us when we get a little too serious about ourselves... even you. If you take something said in here personally, then close the book, and please read the title to yourself out loud.

A Reality Check- Many of us speak our mind with zeal and passion, and we annoy the crap out of others who may not be as zealous or passionate as we are. This book is a reminder for each of us to chill out... to learn to temper our speech, body language and attitudes. The artwork in this book was generated by AI using a picture of ME. I did this so that as I looked at each picture, I'm reminded that I must also learn to give others space, be careful to speak and act with kindness and integrity, and in doing so...
**SHOW OTHERS I REALLY DO CARE!
SO HERE WE GO! LET'S HAVE SOME FUN!**

I demand you call me by my pronouns- I/they/them!

 SERIOUSLY, NO ONE CARES...

I'm a vegan! Animals don't want you to eat them!

YEAH, BUT NO ONE REALLY CARES...

I don't have kids, but I know you should NEVER spank them!

 REALLY? OH WAIT, NO ONE CARES...

Artificial Intelligence is dangerous! It will take over and kill us all!

 AAGH!!! EXCEPT NO ONE CARES…

I believe a woman should be able to have an abortion up to the time of birth!

 BABIES MATTER, NO ONE CARES...

I think the Bible and any mention of God should be removed from our country!

CHILL DUDE, NO ONE CARES...

I think we should cancel anyone who disagrees with our politics!

 OK, GO VOTE BUT NO ONE CARES...

I don't believe churches or religious organizations should be tax exempt!

 RELAX BUBBA, NO ONE CARES...

I think cheerleading and competitive dance should be considered sports!

 GIVE ME A N-O-O-N-E CARES!

I demand college tuition should be free for all, and student loans forgiven!

 CHECKING... UM, NO ONE CARES...

I think we should get rid of Daylight Savings Time forever!

 IT'S "NO ONE CARES" O'CLOCK...

I don't believe the death penalty should be used under any circumstances!

 YOU KILL ME BRO, NO ONE CARES...

I'm in favor of defunding all police and using the money for counseling!

 "911 NO ONE CARES LINE HERE"!

I demand the legal age for drinking, drug use and voting be 16 years old!

 CERTAIN NO ONE OVER 16 CARES...

I insist that we eliminate the Electoral College and elections be popular vote!

 VOTE ON IT OR NO ONE CARES...

I think fracking for energy should be outlawed in the United States!

 WHAT THE FRAK, NO ONE CARES...

I think historic statues of people I disagree with should be torn down!

 NO ONE CARES, EXCEPT BIRDS...

If you care about racism you should kneel during the National Anthem!

HAHA... HAHA...NO ONE CARES...

I believe minimum wage should pay a "living wage" to those working full time!

 A "NO ONE CARES" WITH FRIES...

I believe that healthcare is a right and should be available for free to all!

 IT IS NOW, SO NO ONE CARES...

I believe students in K-12 should be required to wear a school uniform!

 NO HOODIES? NO ONE CARES...

Social media is so bad, there be a should be minimum age of 18 to use it.

 SAY IT LOUDER, NO ONE CARES...

The government has messed up Social Security so bad, it should be privatized.

 TAKE A BREATH... NO ONE CARES...

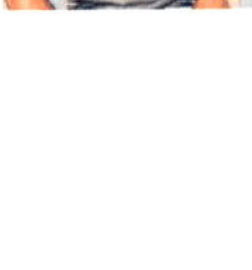

I believe the best thing for all would be to guarantee Universal Basic Income!

 HOW SWEET! NO ONE CARES...

I think zoos are immoral, and it's wrong to keep any animal locked in a cage!

 ARE YOU LION? NO ONE CARES...

I insist the government approve school vouchers for private schools!

 EDUMACATION? NO ONE CARES...

I demand all Jews leave Israel & that a Palestinian state be created now!

 FOR REAL? NO ONE CARES...

It should be legal to assist someone who is terminally ill in committing suicide!

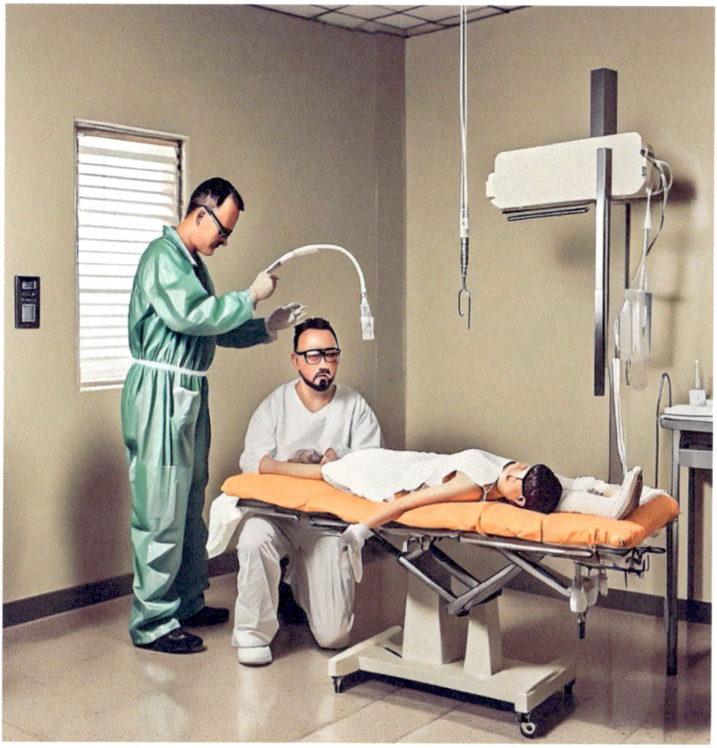

 DEAD SERIOUS... NO ONE CARES...

I don't believe police officers should be allowed to wear body cameras!

 SAY "CHEESE", & NO ONE CARES...

I think the government should be able to set prices for medications!

 SWALLOW THIS... NO ONE CARES...

I think Drag Queen Story time should be allowed for children of all ages!

GO AWAY, NO ONE CARES...

I think MAGA people and President Trump are all losers!

NO ONE CARES TRUMPS THAT...

I only eat naturally grown, Earth-friendly and organic food!

EAT SOME BARK... NO ONE CARES...

There is no reason for anyone to own a gun, especially an AR 15!

#BILLOFRIGHTS... NO ONE CARES...

I believe Socialism is the best way for society to care for its people!

MOVE TO CUBA, NO ONE CARES...

iPhones will always be a better phone and system than an Android!

ilIKE BOTH BRO? NO ONE CARES...

I know that Aliens and lizard people are running the world governments!

EXPLAINS A LOT & NO ONE CARES...

I'm convinced Evolution & Darwinism are the only truths in science!

BAHAHA, YEAH, NO ONE CARES...

I think religion and churches and religious people suck!

~~NO ONE~~ JESUS CARES...

I'm sure that Covid came out of a bat sold in a Chinese market!

ALL JOKES ASIDE, NO ONE CARES...

You assumed my gender!
You assumed my gender!
You assumed my gender!

...I MAY HAVE... & NO ONE CARES...

Reparations should be paid to the descendants of American slaves!

SIMMER DOWN, NO ONE CARES...

I believe healthcare, housing and a basic minimum income should be free!

BURGERS TOO? NO ONE CARES...

In my opinion the United States is not the greatest country in the world!

THEN LEAVE... NO ONE CARES...

Ignoring weather cycles, I still say climate change is a global catastrophe!

SNOW IT ISN'T... NO ONE CARES...

I'm sure that the moon landing was fake! We never landed on the moon ever!

WEIRD, BUT OK? NO ONE CARES...

I know the KING, Elvis, is still alive and living in South America!

VIVA SANTIAGO! NO ONE CARES...

I believe in ghosts, and that you can talk to your deceased loved ones!

REGRETTABLY, NO ONE CARES...

I know that everything about 9/11 was a government conspiracy!

TIN FOIL DUDE... NO ONE CARES...

The Illuminati are moving to take over the world's governments and money!

AND STILL... NO ONE CARES...

I believe if you don't take vaccinations, you are stupid and a threat to society!

STICK YOURSELF... NO ONE CARES...

I think that video games are the cause of all gun violence!

I ASKED MARIO... NO ONE CARES...

I believe no matter what, only white people can be racist!

DISHONEST, BUT NO ONE CARES...

I believe anyone who doesn't believe the Earth is billions of years old is stupid!

ALRIGHTY! BUT NO ONE CARES...

I totally believe in psychics, fortune tellers, astrology, and tarot cards!

THEY KNOW NO ONE CARES?

Intelligent folks know holistic meds are better than modern medicine!

OIL IT, HERB IT... NO ONE CARES...

I know that being a "fur parent" is just as important as having human kids!

EXCEPT NOT... NO ONE CARES...

I believe Bigfoot, Loch Ness, Skinwalkers and Aliens are all real!

NO ONE CARES...YETI DRONES ON...

I'm sure cow farts and coal plants will destroy the planet!

#COWSMUSTFART NO ONE CARES...

I think the polar ice cap and all polar bears will be gone in 10 years!

SINCE THE 1970'S! NO ONE CARES...

I don't care what the dictionary says, the letter "Y" is NOT a vowel!

DOES IT MATTER? NO ONE CARES...

Political correctness should be mandatory, whether you agree or not!

COOL IT BRO, NO ONE CARES...

I vote that PlayStation 2 is the best gaming console of all time!

CHILL GEEKS... NO ONE CARES...

I don't think anyone should be allowed to be a billionaire!

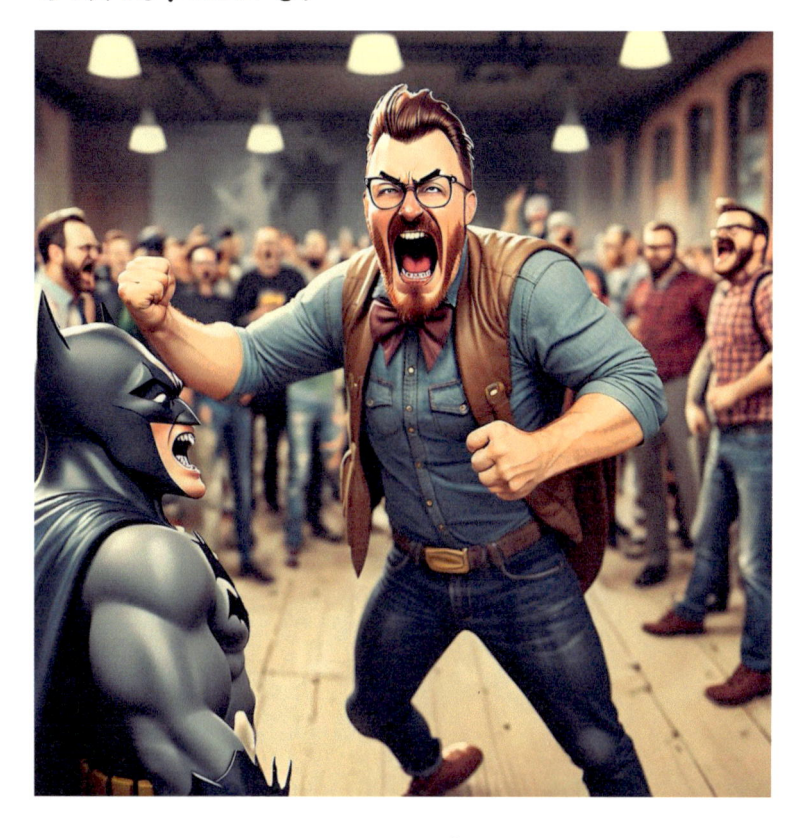

DON'T BE ONE... NO ONE CARES...

I believe there's proof that giving people the "OK" sign is racist!

NO ONE CARES... OTAY?

I know Rick Astley is "Never Gonna Give You Up, OR Let You Down"!

RICK ON A ROLL... NO ONE CARES...

I'll defend a person's right to believe that they are a "furry", a human animal!

STRAIGHT FACE... NO ONE CARES...

I know DC comics and movies are better than Marvel comics and movies!

NO ONE CARES... BUT BE BATMAN!

My pet really does understand what I'm saying!

SURE IT DOES... & NO ONE CARES...

Believe me, Bitcoin is the only currency you should trust!

CRYPTOLICIOUS? NO ONE CARES...

When it comes to burgers, McDonalds is way better than Burger King!

FAST BUT FOOD? NO ONE CARES...

I believe solar & wind are the only acceptable fuels of the future!

BLOW & SHINE... NO ONE CARES...

There are more than two genders! Gender is not static, it is fluid!

NO ONE CARES... #NOTREALITY

I don't care what you say, Coca Cola will always be better than Pepsi!

DR. PEPPER IS! & NO ONE CARES...

Seriously people...

We all have our own set of values, our preferences and our beliefs. Just don't shove, shout, scream or inflict yours on the rest of us!

But you keep being you, Sunshine...

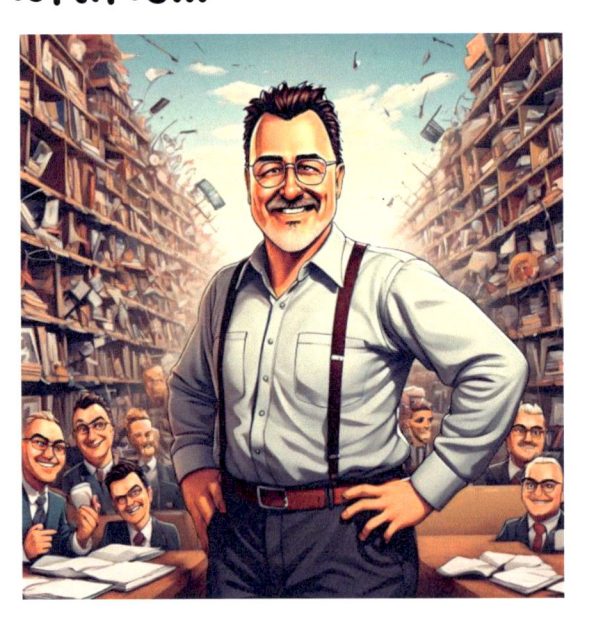

ALL. DAY. LONG.

Made in the USA
Columbia, SC
03 October 2024

45bb92fd-7ff1-4dc8-8a8c-35d64b4b80bfR01